The Far Right and Racism

ADAM HIBBERT

W

FRANKLIN WATTS
LONDON•SYDNEY

First published in 2003 by Franklin Watts
96 Leonard Street, London EC2A 4XD

Franklin Watts Australia
46-51 Huntley Street
Alexandria, NSW 2015

Copyright © Franklin Watts 2003
Series editor: Rachel Cooke
Series design: White Design
Picture research: Diana Morris

A CIP catalogue record for this book is available from the British Library.

ISBN: 0 7496 4882 1

Printed in Belgium

Acknowledgements:
AKG London: 6t © VG BILD-KUNST, Bonn & DACS London 2003, 7t, 14t;
Andy Clark/Reuter/Popperfoto: 10b; Corbis: 4, 6b, 17b, 25tr;
Robert Essel NYC/Corbis: 22t; Leonard Foeger/Reuter/Popperfoto: 26b;
Friends of Kerwin: 9b; Walter Fritz/Reuter/Popperfoto: 17t; Eric Gaillard/Reuter/Popperfoto: 5b;
William Gottlieb/Corbis: 12t; Tom Kidd/Rex Features: 13b; Megan Lewis/Reuter/Popperfoto: 19b;
Richard Oliver/Rex Features: 12b; PA Photos: 23b; Popperfoto: 8b, 9l, 18b; Rex Features: 19t, 27b;
Mike Schroder/Still Pictures: front cover, 16; Sipa Press/Rex Features: 24, 26t, 29t; Rick
Stevens/Reuter/Popperfoto: 25b; Charles Sykes/Rex Features: 11; Ray Tang/Rex Features: 28br; Mike
Theiler/Reuter/Popperfoto: 15b; B. Thomas/Popperfoto: 21b; Tom Wagner/Corbis: 28c; Ian
Waldie/Reuter/Popperfoto: 14b; Michael S. Yamashita/Corbis: 20t.

Whilst every attempt has been made to clear copyright should there be any inadvertent
omission please apply in the first instance to the publisher regarding rectification.

CONTENTS

A POLITICAL PARTY promotes one set of ideas about how to run society. In the 20th century, parties became known as right wing or left wing, according to their attitudes to business and the economy. Roughly, the left wanted to steer the economy so that money was shared more equally between rich and poor. The right wanted to free the economy from most controls, believing this would create more money for everyone. This was a battle between socialism and the free market.

⬆ Police try to contain a mob led by far right agitators who forced 200 immigrants to leave their hostel in Rostock, Germany in 1992.

↘ In 2002 the world was shocked when far right leader Le Pen was runner-up in the French presidential elections.

RADICAL POLITICS

Radical groups exist at both extremes of this range of political ideas. Far left radicals – communists – believe that the economy cannot avoid being unfair. For them, equality can only be won by a workers' revolution. Far right parties – fascists – believe that most social problems are the fault of the left. They also believe radical change is necessary. Far right groups in different countries express this in different ways. However, the strongest common theme among far right groups around the world is an interest in racial politics.

THE FAR RIGHT AND RACE

Modern far right politics are closely connected with conspiracy theories about Jewish people. Most far right groups believe that humanity is divided into races, like animal species, which should be kept apart. Whenever racial politics have become popular, minority groups have been persecuted. When the German far right – the National Socialist or Nazi party – was in power in the 1930s and 40s, it ordered the round-up and extermination of Europe's Jews. Millions were gassed or starved to death in labour camps. More recently, these ideas evolved into more general campaigns against foreigners "stealing our jobs".

RIGHT NOW

The far right lost popularity when the Nazis' crimes were exposed after the Second World War. There was a brief interest in far right ideas in the 1970s, at a time of economic crisis, but far right ideas rarely appeared in serious politics. In the first years of the 21st century, the far right had some election successes which caused a lot of experts to worry that voters were once again turning to the far right.

MADRID 1936

¡NO PASARAN! ¡PASAREMOS!
Sie kommen nicht durch! Wir kommen durch!

This left-wing Spanish Civil War poster shows the enemy as vultures, wearing the badges of Nazism and Fascism.

THE FIRST WORLD WAR began a crisis around the world. The war was followed by a disastrous flu epidemic, and a workers' revolution in Russia which set up a system of common ownership – communism. This new system looked like a deadly rival to Western economies as they struggled through hard times in the 1920s and 30s.

LEFT AND RIGHT FIGHT

Far right groups gained popularity by blaming outsiders for Europe's problems. They were very tough on leftists, and this appealed to people who were worried about the spread of communism from Russia. In Spain in the late 1930s, the far right Falange group led a military coup against a left wing government. They were backed by arms and air support from the German Nazis and Italian Fascists.

Justice Oliver Wendell Holmes, the US judge who ruled that Carrie Buck should be sterilised. Summing up, he said: "Three generations of imbeciles are enough."

RACES APART

Many moderate countries were grateful to these far right governments for their efforts to stop the far left. The overt racism, particularly of the Nazis, was also tolerated. It was fashionable in the early 20th century to believe that some people were more evolved than other people (see panel). This "scientific racism" provided an easy explanation for inequality in society. It seemed to explain why social status should pass from parent to child. Some countries tried eugenics – breeding "better" people by preventing some from having children. In 1927, single mother Carrie Buck was the first of about 60,000 Americans to be involuntarily sterilised by law in the USA.

↑ *A 15th-century woodcut shows a group of Jews being burnt alive by Christians.*

FACING THE ISSUES

Many far right supporters believe in "the Aryan race". The idea comes from Count de Gobineau, a French aristocrat writing in the mid-19th century. He argued that Europe's richest families came from the Aryan race, one separate from the mass of "common" people. Gobineau's Aryans were paler, more intelligent and natural leaders. Gobineau's "scientific" idea of a superior race of aristocrats was not popular at first. It became fashionable as other thinkers changed the idea to include all Europeans, not just the upper classes. Poor white people were given a reason to feel special.

MONEY LENDERS

Christian countries, too, had a history of hatred towards Jewish minorities. In feudal times, the ban in the Bible against lending money (usury) was taken seriously by Christians. But loans provided merchants with a vital tool, and non-Christian groups such as Jews were encouraged to lend them money. Jewish communities were often massacred or driven from a country, especially when important people decided not to pay their debts.

THE NAZIS

With the Second World War, attitudes to the far right were to change dramatically. The far right's success in Germany rested on the Nazi's promise to restore German pride, after the losses of the First World War. Germany invaded other countries, and began exterminating "enemies" of the Aryan race – Jews, gay men, gypsies and disabled people – within its expanding borders.

AFTER THE HOLOCAUST

WHEN GERMANY was defeated at the end of the Second World War, the world learned what had happened to Jewish people under Nazi rule – the mass murder of millions of men, women and children, in what is now known as the Holocaust. Racial politics were clearly to blame.

GONE BUT NOT FORGOTTEN

The Allied victors hanged Nazi leaders for crimes against humanity, and established the United Nations to promote equality and human rights for all. But this sudden change in mainstream ideas did not convince everyone. A few stayed loyal to the ideas of the Nazis. Some decided that Allied claims about Nazi crimes were made-up, to make their victory seem more important (see page 15). Many still believed that other "races" were inferior to them – if not the Jews, then those with darker skins. Black citizens were still harassed in most Western countries.

IMPERIAL DREAMS

The greatest non-European empire, Japan, also had difficulty accepting its new status, as it was occupied by the American army and governed by an American military official. Many Japanese people had fond memories of the pre-war era, when Japan could think of itself as the leading power in the region, ruled by a holy emperor.

WHAT DO YOU THINK?

During Nazi persecution of the Jews before the war, Jewish refugees were often turned away by other Western countries. After the war, the UN's Universal Declaration of Human Rights was adopted in December, 1948. The 14th article of the Declaration says: "Everyone has the right to seek and to enjoy in other countries asylum from persecution."

- Should all migrants be welcomed into a country? If not, why not?
  - Should countries accept refugees?
  - Would you have sent Jewish refugees back to Nazi Germany? Why do you think some countries did this?
  - Today, to gain asylum – refugee status – people must prove that they have "well-founded fear of persecution" in their home country. Why do you think this might be hard for an asylum seeker to prove?

*The writer Yukio Mishima became an icon of the Japanese far right's dreams of old imperial glory. He committed **seppuku** – ritual suicide – in 1970.*

THE COLD WAR

The post-war era saw a new contest between Western countries, led by the USA, and communist Russia. This "cold war" caused upheaval in many countries, as both sides gave help to left or right wing groups in civil wars. With improved transport links, and the need to rebuild the international economy, many more people migrated across the world to escape civil war or to find work in industrialised countries.

ECONOMIC CRISIS RETURNS

Unemployment rose rapidly in the recession of the 1970s. Far right groups made the most of the crisis, blaming immigrant labour for the shortage of jobs. Developed countries brought in laws to limit migration, seeming to agree with the far right's argument. By campaigning on race, mainstream parties stole support from the far right, whose popularity shrank once more.

⬅ *Jamaican immigrants arrive in the UK in 1952. The British government asked them to move to Britain to help rebuild the economy after the devastation of war.*

➡ *This young Dutchman, Kerwin, was beaten to death in 1983 by a man with "100% white" tatooed on his arm. Kerwin is still remembered in a famous poem.*

THE FINAL COLLAPSE *of the communist bloc of countries at the end of the 1980s marked the end of the Cold War. The "free market" of capitalism had won the day. There now seemed to be little point to left wing or right wing politics. All parties had to rethink their ideas to appeal to voters in these new circumstances. Far right groups argued, split, and reformed in new types.*

NONE OF THE ABOVE

Most developed countries in the 1990s saw a sharp drop in the number of people who participated in public life. Membership of political parties fell, and so did voter turn-out at elections. The effect was also felt more widely, for example in church congregations, sporting associations, hobby groups and charities. In the US, membership of voluntary associations as diverse as the Red Cross and bowling leagues has dropped by between 25% and 50% in the last thirty years. This disinterest in public life and ideas hit membership numbers of far right groups, too.

GET THE FACTS STRAIGHT

These statistics show the percentage of people who used their vote in the past few elections:

- Denmark assembly elections: (1987) 85.9%, (1988) 82.7%, (1990) 80.4%, (1994) 81.7%, (1998) 83.1%.
- France assembly elections: (1986) 69.9%, (1988) 58.1%, (1993) 61.3%, (1997) 59.9% .
- Netherlands assembly: (1986) 84.2%, (1989) 78.0%, (1994) 75.2%, (1998) 70.1% .
- UK parliamentary elections: (1987) 75.3%, (1992) 77.7%, (1997) 71.5%, (2001) 59%.
- USA presidential elections: (1988) 50.1%, (1992) 55.2%, (1996) 49.0%, (2000) 51.0%.

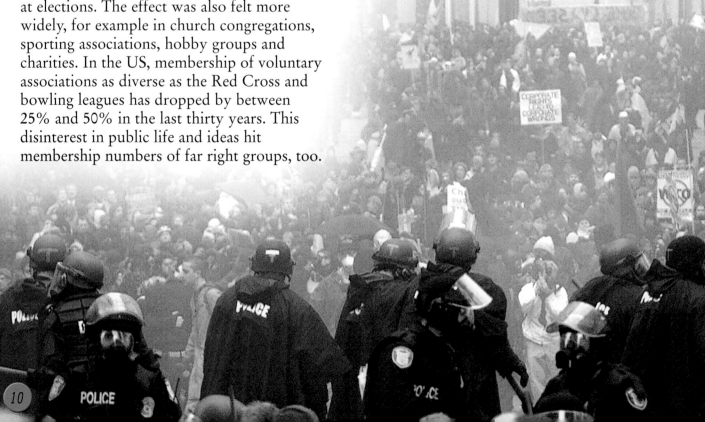

ALONE AND AFRAID

As individuals withdrew from public life, they cared less about people in other walks of life, and about changes in the world around them. People became less welcoming towards strangers, and less trusting of experts in fields such as scientific research. The far right picked up on this fear of the unknown. It began to campaign on the "risks" posed by unfamiliar minorities, such as Muslims.

GLOBAL BUSINESS

The "victory" of capitalism meant that business could cross all national boundaries. Some people worried that global businesses had become more powerful than nations, weakening democracy. Protests began against "globalisation". Far right groups believe in strong nations, and some claim that international business is controlled by a conspiracy of Jewish people. So the far right, as well as the far left, got involved in anti-globalisation campaigns.

POPULAR APPEAL

By the year 2000, most far right movements had made big changes to their politics. They stopped talking about racial politics openly, and concentrated on voters' sense that politicians were ignoring them. Far right activists got involved in single-issue campaigns, such as defending farmers or animal rights. They criticised mainstream politicians for being too distant from the realities of everyday life.

→ The floodlight memorial for the World Trade Center. Its destruction in 2001 by Islamic terrorists gave far right groups a chance to attack Muslim minorities.

← The "anti-globalisation" protests in Seattle, shown here, and elsewhere have been supported by some far right groups.

UNLIKE SOME LEFT WING and environmental political groups, the far right rarely organises internationally. Each country has its own far right traditions and beliefs. The racial policies of different groups, even within the same country, may target different minority groups. There are more common themes than racial politics, though.

⬆ Most people take pride in the traditions of their country, such as saluting the flag. Nationalism takes this idea further.

FOR MY COUNTRY

The far right is nationalist – they are devoted to their own country, and approve of almost anything they think is in their nation's interests. The far right aim to defend their own nation's free choice – its sovereignty – against outside forces such as the United Nations, foreign economic interests or cultural influences from abroad.

NO NONSENSE

The far right believes that people enjoy too many rights and civil liberties – that the state should be given more power to police and punish crime, for example. The far right often disapproves of the idea of women's rights. It encourages women to take up their "natural" role as mothers and home-makers. The German Nazi party took away the freedom to be a mother, controlling which women could have children.

⬅ This sign on a South African beach banned black people from sharing it with the whites – a result of the racist policy of Apartheid of its whites-only government.

➡ Southern USA, with it history of slavery, is home to a racist terror group, the Klu Klux Klan. Members mask their faces to carry out racist harrassment, murders and terrorism.

SEPARATE DEVELOPMENT

The far right believes that races should be kept apart – as happened during South Africa's Apartheid era (1948–91). Modern far right parties do not use directly racial language – only a few claim that some races are superior to others. Instead, to seem more fair and open-minded, they use the language of multiculturalism, talking in terms of promoting the culture and ethnic identity of white people.

UNNATURAL BEHAVIOUR

Most far right groups believe that humanity should respect nature and follow nature's lead. People who don't fit their definition of what is natural – the disabled, gay men and lesbians – are targeted. Far right American politician Pat Buchanan often described the AIDS epidemic among gay people in the 1980s as nature's punishment for their "unnatural" lifestyle.

WHAT DO YOU THINK?

What do you think of these quotes from far right groups? Are they talking about race or ethnic identity? Is there a difference?

- "Every race needs a homeland, even the white race. Our culture is just as valid as the 'native american indian' or the Chinese or the black culture." White Truth

- "The Politically Correct (though scientifically incorrect) liberal position is that the only difference between black people and white people is 'skin colour'." British National Party

- "We demand an immediate and total halt to all illegal immigration, and a careful screening of legal immigrants, to select those who can fit into the American way of life and contribute to the well-being of our society." whitecivilrights.com

THOUGH RACIAL discrimination is outlawed in most countries, racial prejudices are still widely-held. However, there is one type of racism, anti-Semitism (hatred of Jewish people), that is closely associated with far right politics.

AGAINST JEWS

Whether Jewish communities live apart or try to integrate with host communities, they have been attacked. Reasons for hating Jews can only be found in the minds of anti-Semites, not in how Jewish people live. Anti-Semites need outsiders, or scapegoats, to blame for social problems. Without scapegoats, the far right would have to treat social problems as the fault of its own people – a much less popular idea.

⬇ *Vandalism at a synagogue in Britain. The swastika – the Nazi symbol – indicates the vandal's support of the Holocaust.*

⬆ *This Nazi propaganda cartoon portrays Jewish men as rich, ugly and secretive. It was designed to make poor Germans feel angry and jealous.*

IT'S A CONSPIRACY

Anti-Semitism, unlike other forms of racism, is a type of conspiracy theory. It believes that Jewish people plot amongst themselves to make other races weaker, and to control societies. Some far right groups believe that Jewish people encourage "whites" to have children with other races, to weaken the Aryan race. Extremists call their imaginary secret conspiracy the Zionist Occupation Government (ZOG).

FACING THE ISSUES

The far right often tries to prove that the German Nazi party was not as guilty of mass murder - genocide - as most people believe. This is known as Holocaust Denial. It takes three main paths: denying that any Jewish people at all were murdered, or arguing over the number of Jewish people murdered, or denying that Nazi leaders knew what was happening in the camps. Some have even claimed that the famous diary of Anne Frank, a young Jewish girl who died in the camps, is a forgery. It is in the far right's interests to confuse people about the Holocaust. As long as we are sure that it took place, it remains proof of the horror of far right racism.

FINAL SOLUTION

The German Nazi party was the only far right group to gain enough power to put anti-Semitism fully into practice. As well as regulating motherhood, it began other programmes to try to make "Aryan" Germans healthier and stronger. It blamed Jewish conspirators for Germany's defeat in the First World War, rounding them up into ghettos, and eventually moving millions to camps to be murdered.

BLACK ANTI-SEMITISM

The main non-white group to believe in racial segregation, Louis Farrakhan's Nation of Islam, is also anti-Semitic. Like far right groups with white supporters, Farrakhan's organisation blames Jews for the low status of black people in the USA and around the world. It has little to do with mainstream Muslim beliefs.

Louis Farrakhan proclaims his message. His young black followers – the Fruits of Islam – adopt military style habits and uniforms.

15

DIFFERENT COUNTRIES *have different rules about far right political activities. In Germany, for example, some Nazi symbols and even arguments are banned. In others, such as Spain and the USA, all political comment is legal, however much it offends some people.*

⬇ *A neo-Nazi group marches in Germany. They are forbidden to carry the Nazis' original symbol of the swastika, but their militaristic style of uniform is clearly adopted from them.*

GOING LEGIT

Far right parties with a reputation for violence and mad ideas have to go through a difficult process to convince voters that they are sensible politicians. As a result, far right groups tend to split their activities into two "wings". A political wing campaigns for votes, while a more secretive group carries out racist attacks and vandalism. Some party leaders decide they want a more legitimate status so they persuade their members to concentrate on being respectable. This has cost some far right parties their most active members, who leave to form more radical groups. Reformed far right groups encourage women to join to help them promote a family image.

One Austrian far right party changed into a "mainstream" party under the guidance of Jorg Haider. Here he poses with a bear in a crowd-pleasing publicity shot.

JUNIOR PARTNERS

In countries where parliamentary seats are given in line with the total number of votes for each party, "respectable" far right groups may sometimes win enough seats to gain some power. Often a mainstream party cannot form a government without finding allies, so a far right group could be invited to form a coalition with the larger party and gain a say in government. This has happened recently in Italy and Austria.

THE HARDCORE

Some far right activists are most interested in direct action, intimidating or attacking immigrants and other "enemies" of the cause such as gay men. They are not as interested in elections and voters, but may act as bodyguards or stewards for far right politicians and events. These gangs sometimes set up their own groups.

HATE ON THE WEB

The openness of the internet allows all sorts of people to form "virtual" political groups. Far right parties have used the technology to reach people who might not hear about them otherwise – and lets those people feel involved, even if they are isolated in their community. This also makes far right groups easier to monitor.

FACING THE ISSUES

TJ Leyden (below) is an ex-US marine who was recruited by the White Supremacy Movement as a teenager. It took him 15 years of beating people up, recruiting other thugs, and teaching racism to his own children before he realised that he had to get out. His wife stayed in the movement and divorced him. Leyden now works with the Simon Wiesenthal Centre (see page 26) teaching young men about the tricks and lies far right extremists use to convince them to join the cause.

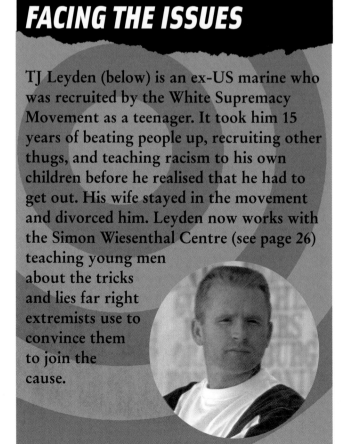

PROPAGANDA

AN IMPORTANT PART of any political group's activities is making and distributing propaganda – information designed to win people over to the group's ideas.

Propaganda is usually a genuine, honest statement of what the group believes, but some groups will use lies and false rumours to trick people into supporting them.

INVENTING THE TECHNIQUES

Far right groups have been skilled at propaganda from their earliest days. They were clever at creating false information: an early success was a book which pretended to be a list of the aims of an international Jewish conspiracy (which didn't exist). The German Nazis recognised the power of the new forms of communication that had appeared in the 20th century, and used posters, films and the radio very effectively. Radio was a new medium then, like the internet today. They used these media to build up the almost god-like status of their leader, Adolf Hitler.

SETTING OUT THEIR STALL

At elections and some other occasions, parties write down what they believe, and what they will do if you vote them into power. It is called a manifesto. The new far right parties have to pick their words carefully in their manifesto. If it is too clearly racist, voters will be offended. But if it is too "soft" on racial issues, the membership of the party will not agree with it.

WHAT DO YOU THINK?

If far right politicians believe that racial segregation is a good thing, and want to try to persuade the voters to elect them on the strength of that idea, why should they be stopped? Are they to blame if a member of the audience conducts a racist attack afterwards?

Would you:
a) Ban them all?
b) Give them a fair hearing at a debate?
c) Allow them to broadcast an election advert?
d) Make no restrictions at all?

⬆ *These protesters want to show people at a far right meeting that their ideas are unacceptable.*

MEDIA MANAGEMENT

With smaller memberships, political parties are more dependent on the media to get their message across than ever before. They lack the numbers of campaigners needed to go from door to door and talk to each voter. Modern far right parties are beginning to manage their relationships with the media more carefully, setting up teams of experts who keep an eye on the news for opportunities to put their ideas to the public.

⬅ *The British Union of Fascist's propaganda chief, William Joyce, speaking in the 1930s. The German Nazi party recruited him to broadcast propaganda on the radio to Britain during the war.*

FREE SPEECH - ONE EACH

Media in different countries have different rules about what to report, especially in political contests such as elections. The normal rules allow every party an equal amount of time to state their case, but far right groups may be left out. Leaders of far right parties who state clearly what they believe in may be prosecuted for encouraging people to be violent to minorities.

⬅ *The Australian right wing leader, Pauline Hanson (right), brought her ideas to viewers on this daytime TV chat show – a controversial move which gained her further publicity.*

WHILE POLITICAL ACTIVITY fell in the 1990s, young consumers took more care over the music and clothes that they bought to express themselves. The 1970s image of the far right as working class, tough and rebellious gained popularity as a sort of fashion statement. A new "far right" music scene took off around the world.

GIVE ME STRENGTH

The followers of this new "scene" had little interest in politics, just enjoying its words and styles for their ability to shock. Like punk music in the 1970s, it offered young consumers a new self image. By adopting the clothes, angry attitude and music of extremist bands such as Skrewdriver and No Remorse, they could join the "gang". Instead of feeling helpless or useless, they could feel powerful and united. Secret codes, such as 18 for <u>A</u>dolf <u>H</u>itler or 88 for <u>H</u>eil <u>H</u>itler, help make them feel part of the club.

⬆ *The Union Jack flag became a punk rock icon, and teenage rebels around the world wore it as a simple fashion statement.*

SHAKE YOUR MONEY MAKER

Far right music since the 1970s has been closely linked to far right political groups. It raised funds for them from record sales, brought new young people to the scene for political activists to recruit, and provided a space where far right fantasies could be expressed. But record labels such as Blood & Honour became independent in the late 80s, breaking official links with far right parties.

NO REMORSE

BARBECUE IN ROSTOCK

⬅ *This music CD celebrates a racist arson attack in Rostock (see page 4), in which several Turkish people were burnt to death.*

➡ *Some of these football fans use "Hitler salutes" to offend rival fans. Does this make them Nazis? Or are they just being part of the gang?*

ULTRA-VIOLENCE

Some fans of far right music and the lifestyle around it join in racist attacks and other forms of anti-social activity for fun, rather than politics. Like violence in and around bars or in crowds of sports fans, this criminal activity is enjoyed for the "buzz" and as an "adventure" to laugh about with friends afterwards. It is not always evidence of deeply-held far right opinions, though victims of such attacks might not notice the difference.

SKINHEADS

The skinhead subculture is often associated with the far right and racist violence. But it began with "ska" music and the enjoyment of West Indian (black) music, and most skinheads are not followers of racial politics. Skinheads Against Racial Prejudice (SHARP) is an association which tries to remind the media and other skinheads of their subculture's non-racist roots.

GET THE FACTS STRAIGHT

These are just a few of the labels and bands that have gained notoriety for their far right links.

- Skrewdriver: Lead singer broke from British far right to form Blood & Honour label.
- Blood & Honour: Financed C-18, the Europe-wide Nazi punk terror organisation.
- ISD records: Another C-18 business.
- Intimidation One: US far right band from Oregon.
- No Remorse: Operates from the same postal address as British far right National Socialist Alliance.
- Svastika: Swedish Nazi band.
- NS88 & NS Records: Run by Marcel Schilf, C-18 figure in Denmark, until his death in 2001.
- Resistance Records: Canadian "hate core" label bought by American fascist William Pearce.
- Nordland Records: Swedish label taken-over by American fascist William Pearce.
- Nordic Fest: Musical fundraising event for Imperial Klans of America, a white power group.

⬆ *The far right gains most support in places where reliable jobs, such as in this factory, are in short supply.*

FAR RIGHT GROUPS *offer simple solutions and appeal to popular myths, especially about immigrants. This "straight-talking" appeals to people who are impatient with the careful and detailed treatment of issues by mainstream politicians. It is normal sometimes to feel that life has treated you unfairly. Far right beliefs can give this idea a political expression, focusing people's anger onto minorities.*

I AM NOT A LOSER

Unemployed men have most reason to welcome far right ideas. Unemployment makes people feel left out, unwanted and powerless. A lack of jobs is due to the way the global economy works, which few individuals can do anything about – making them feel even more powerless. Far right ideas pin the blame on "outsiders" living locally – minority groups. This provides a clear target to "fight back" against, to regain self-respect.

LEFT TO RIGHT

The far right also recruits people from urban communities which traditionally supported the left wing, or labour unions. Unions and left wing parties once believed that working people should act together to force employers to give them a better standard of living. As left wing leaders became more friendly to employers in the 1980s and 90s, some felt that the far right was more "socialist" than their old leaders.

GET THE FACTS STRAIGHT

The far right gains most of its support from people who assume that minorities and migrants are being given unfair advantages, allowed to get away with crime, and to cost "white" taxpayers money. Here are some facts which do not support these popular prejudices:

- Australian Income:
  Below $12,000: 64% Aborigine, 45% of others.
  Above $35,000: 2% Aborigine, 11% of others.

- British immigrant contribution: In 1999-2000, immigrants in Britain added £2.5 billion more value to the economy than they consumed. (UK Treasury figures)

- Share of care for refugees by industrial countries: In 1999 Tanzania received more refugees than the whole of Europe put together. Up to 70% of the world's refugees remain within the region of their country, especially in the Middle East and Africa.

- On treatment of criminals: Black–Americans, who make up 12% of the US population and 13% of its drug users, are 35% of all those arrested for drug possession, 55% of those convicted of possession, and 74% of those sent to prison for possession. (Bureau of Justice statistics, 1993)

ECCENTRIC INTELLECTUALS

Some far right members are wealthy and well educated. Many try out several different types of political groups before joining the far right. Some are first interested by revisionism – history which defends the record of German Nazis. Other intellectual routes to the far right come from sociobiology (the study of human culture as a product of evolution) and some "New Age" or environmentalist ideas.

HERE FOR THE BEER

Some far right supporters are more interested in being part of a gang than in politics. They enjoy the "team spirit" of meetings, campaigns and socialising with like-minded people. They are more likely to be involved in violence, murder and vandalism than the more political members.

⬇ *This British far right politician was working for a Japanese manufacturer when she was elected a local councillor in 2002. Global business is sometimes blamed by the far right for local unemployment.*

A French farmers' protest in Rouen. The far right has tried to attract voters from dissatisfied groups such as this.

THE MORE MAINSTREAM the far right becomes, the more voters it can appeal to. Most modern far right political parties are very careful to talk about ethnicity instead of race, to avoid seeming too extreme. They may also try to focus campaigns on issues such as crime and jobs. But members do not want their party to become just another right wing mainstream party, so nationalism and racism are always present in one form or another.

WHITES WITH AMBITION

Some people vote for the far right in the hope of making life better for themselves and their children. They are convinced by the far right's argument that they are being held back by programmes to help minorities, such as positive discrimination. By voting for the far right, they want to put pressure on the government to give them some help as well.

HAPPIER DAYS

Some older people are upset by our louder, busier and more chaotic modern life. The far right's respect for a country's traditions, its flag and the old sense of duty and orderliness can appeal to these people. Veterans of army life and people who served their country in wars are more likely to find the far right's patriotism appealing. Older people who were once moderate right-wingers are also more open to far right ideas.

FACING THE ISSUES

Recently, many governments have toughened their laws on who can enter their countries and claim asylum. These moves support the belief that most asylum seekers are bogus and just want to exploit the economic benefits of being in another country. Governments claim these laws help stop racist violence, yet statistics show that in reality racist violence normally rises after harsh laws against immigrants are introduced. Governments are accused of following racist policies in order to gain votes.

The media may also use race issues to boost sales: in June 2001, the UN's official for refugees wrote that the media in Austria, Italy, Denmark, Australia and Britain were particularly guilty of promoting racial violence. He noted that statistics "are frequently manipulated, facts are taken out of context, and the character of asylum seekers as a group is often distorted in order to present them as a terrible threat".

⬆ Pia Kjaersgaard, Danish leader of the extreme right, is greeted by elderly supporters waving the Danish flag.

SWEARING AT TEACHER

A large number of voters use the far right as a protest vote – a way to shock and offend mainstream politicians who they feel are ignoring their needs. The more this group is told that voting for the far right is wrong, the more protest voters can be sure that their vote for the far right will upset the political elite. They may know little and care less about what the far right actually stands for.

⬇ Like thousands around the world, this Muslim asylum seeker in Australia has been detained until he can prove his right to asylum.

ANTI-FASCISM

SOME PEOPLE *take the threat of the far right very seriously, setting up campaign groups to keep an eye on them. They may try to interfere with the far right's ability to organise, by disrupting meetings, planting spies in far right groups and reporting any criminal activity they discover to the police.*

SIMON WIESENTHAL CENTRE

One of the leading Jewish organisations concerned with the far right is the Simon Wiesenthal Centre. Simon Wiesenthal and his wife survived the Holocaust, though almost a hundred of their relatives were killed in Nazi camps. After the war, Wiesenthal dedicated his life to bringing escaped Nazi war criminals to justice. The Centre now focuses on defending the memory of the Holocaust and on monitoring far right groups.

⬆ *A far right supporter is arrested after attempting to shoot the French president. He had previously boasted of his bravery on the C-18 website.*

SEARCHLIGHT

The Searchlight organisation in Britain was formed in 1962 to combat far right organisations. In its first few years it had some big successes, using doubters within the British far right to spy on its activities. Searchlight publishes a newsletter, and still organises campaigns to disrupt and protest at far right events. It is linked with similiar organisations all over the world.

⬅ *Simon Wiesenthal has brought several escaped Nazi war criminals to justice.*

➡ *These tributes are for the 19 children who died, along with 149 office workers, in a "lone bomber" attack in Oklahoma, USA.*

WEB WATCHERS

Many individuals and groups set up pages on the internet to raise awareness of the far right threat in their own countries or around the world. Some of them are listed on page 31. Some are simply information, to help visitors recognise far right activity in their own neighbourhood. Others make fun of some of the sillier aspects of far right groups, or have their own political message.

CONTAINING TERROR

A string of individual acts of terrorism by far right supporters has made authorities around the world take the threat of the far right more seriously. Some far right leaders urge would-be terrorists to break all links with parties and groups, so that their leaders can deny responsibility. Police forces are having to deal with sneak attacks by "lone wolf" bombers or shooters, inspired by far right ideas.

WHAT DO YOU THINK?

Should governments do more to combat far right groups? Or could heavy policing and censorship encourage far right supporters to feel that their cause is being treated unfairly? Here are some other options:

- Change laws which treat immigrants as a threat.
- Promote the ideals of the UN Human Rights Declaration, and the need for asylum.
- Force minorities to be more integrated with a country's culture, for example, learning the language.
- Spend more on spying on far right extremists and prosecuting people who break laws.
- Stop immigration, to make voters less afraid of changes to their communities.

What effect would each of these options have? Could any of them backfire?

THE FAR RIGHT *gains support whenever people feel bitter about how society has treated them. This feeling can grow when politics seem too remote from the people. But the trend in most countries is for less participation in politics and other public activities. Will mainstream politicians or extremists be the first to find a way to involve voters in politics again?*

PROSPERITY IN THE WEST

The great economic slump of the 1930s made far right ideas much more popular than they have been since. The world economy has not grown strongly since the 1980s, but economic conditions in the West have been good for all but the poorest people. Far right ideas are more likely to gain popularity in countries which have suffered real economic hardship, such as Russia or Argentina.

MUDDLING ALONG

Today, the trend in politics is away from strong political beliefs, towards the everyday tasks of government. This has mixed effects on the far right. People are more suspicious of the far right's big ideas. But there are also fewer controversial politicians to make the news exciting, so the media are tempted to give the far right more space.

⬆ *The prosperity that fills busy shops around the developed world, like this one in Tokyo, Japan, also means people are less attracted to political extremes.*

➡ *People will protest against risks and the unknown, such as these young people taking action against GM crops.*

Shocked by Le Pen's success in the presidential elections, French youths protested against him in huge numbers in 2002.

RISK AVOIDANCE

Suspicions about strangers and other potential "risks" (see page 11) give new opportunities to the far right. More people dismiss the advice of experts, such as scientists, believing that it is corrupted by the greed of big business. The far right shares many of these beliefs. It can give people a way to express the fear that we are being put at risk by corrupt authorities.

TALKING UP THE PROBLEM

As the public retreat from political life, politicians are less confident about being in touch with voters. Their insecurity can cause them to take trivial election results far too seriously. But once the far right is discussed as a serious threat, voters may be influenced to treat the far right as a real option. As yet, this effect has not been strong enough for far right groups to use it to build up their memberships.

GET THE FACTS STRAIGHT

In the French presidential election in 2002, the Front National leader, Jean-Marie Le Pen, was voted through to a run-off between him and another right wing candidate, who won the final round. Political experts were horrified by the first result, but these statistics suggest their shock was an over-reaction.

- French Presidential vote, April 2002: Le Pen, Front National 16%.

- French presidential vote, 1995: Le Pen, Front National 15%.

- French assembly elections vote, June 2002: Front National 11% – 0 elected.

- French assembly elections vote, 1997: Front National 15% – 1 elected.

- French assembly elections vote, 1986: Front National 10% – 35 elected.

GLOSSARY

anti-Semitism: The hatred of Jews (Semites).

asylum seeker: A person asking to live in a new country to escape persecution in their own country.

capitalism: A type of economy in which businesses aim to make a profit for the people who own them (whose money provides "the capital").

communism: An alternative to capitalism, in which business aims are set by the people working in them.

civil liberties: Protections which stop the state gaining too much power over citizens.

coalition: A group of countries or organisations working together for a specific goal.

economy: The business life of a nation or group of nations, seen as a whole.

ethnic identity: Shared cultural traditions and origins.

eugenics: The idea that science can improve the human race by controlling who has children.

far right: Describes political groups linked by a belief in very powerful government and racial division.

free market: An economy in which business is run with little or no state interference and so provides for social needs.

genocide: Planned mass murder of a race or nation of people.

globalisation: The trend towards one global economy and society.

Holocaust: The mass murder of Jews and others by the Nazis during the Second World War.

immigrant: A person who arrives in a new country with the aim of making it a home.

left wing: Describes political ideas that suggest that capitalism treats people unequally, and should be controlled.

multiculturalism: An attitude of supporting different cultural groups in one society.

nationalism: A strong belief in the importance of an independent nation state.

politically correct: Following a code of conduct in an attempt to avoid being discriminatory or offensive.

positive discrimination: Policies which try to make up for past inequality by favouring disadvantaged groups.

propaganda: Media produced by a political group to persuade people to give it their support.

racism: The belief that certain genetic characteristics, such as skin colour, define a person.

repatriation: Returning a person to a country they have left, normally by force.

right wing: Describes political ideas that believe the economy should be free of government controls.

socialism: A milder form of communism, which places some of the economy under state control.

society: A country, community or group of people, organised according to certain rules.

sovereignty: The independent authority of a ruler or state over its own land and people.

union: An association formed by working people to defend or improve their status at work.

war crime: An act of inhumanity during war, normally against civilians or prisoners.

Zionist: A person or group devoted to the religious ideal of a Jewish homeland in Israel.

FURTHER INFORMATION

The websites listed here will help you look further into this subject. We have not listed the websites of openly far right organisations because most people find their content offensive. You may want to consider this decision in the light of the "free speech" debate discussed on pages 18/19.

INTER-GOVERNMENTAL ORGANISATIONS

The European Monitoring Centre on Racism and Xenophobia
www.eumc.at
Set up by the EU to study hate groups and racism, and to advise EU members on responses.

The International Organisation for Migration
www.iom.int
Set up by governments around the world to coordinate migration and ensure that it has a positive outcome for all.

Office of the High Commissioner for Human Rights
www.unhchr.ch
Human rights archives, with the text of the Declaration on the Elimination of All Forms of Racial Discrimination, UN resolution 1904, made in 1963.

The United Nations
www.un.org/WCAR
Site about the latest UN anti-racism conference, with access to serious research material.

www.un.org/Pubs/CyberSchoolBus
These are dedicated pages for school students providing an accessible route to UN information, especially their human rights resource.

NON-GOVERNMENTAL ORGANISATIONS

The Anti-Defamation League
www.adl.org
Works to raise awareness of issues far right groups try to confuse people about, including a Hate Symbols database.

Centre for New Community
www.newcomm.org
This Canadian group works to expose far right campaigners as they try to take over other people's issues. See their article on anti-globalisation protests.

Crosspoint Anti-Racism
www.magenta.nl/crosspoint/
This archive, based in the Netherlands, carries links for all the major anti-racist organisations in almost every country of the world.

The Institute for Historical Review
www.ihr.org
This controversial organisation claims to have no political allegiances. It publishes "revisionist" views of 20th century history, including Holocaust Denial stories.

Southern Poverty Law Centre
www.tolerance.org/maps/hate
This resource offers good insights into the state of the far right in the USA.

Searchlight
www.searchlightmagazine.com
The online magazine of this anti-fascist organisation (see page 26).

The Stephen Roth Institute
www.tau.ac.il/Anti-Semitism
Offers a great resource for researching anti-Semitism around the world.

The Wiesenthal Centre
www.wiesenthal.com
Along with information about its work and activities (see page 26), this site also offers resources on aspects of racial prejudice, particularly anti-Semetism.

xborder
antimedia.net/xborder
An example of an activist group from Australia, which encourages people to combat race hate directly by assisting asylum seekers and refugees.

INDEX